Giggles

of

Nature

... and Other Curious Wonders

by Carol A. Castagna

Dedication

To my dear great grandson, Max, his smile, the product of a giggle rising in his eyes, from his heart, before the expression reaches his lips. Bright as the morning sun, like his mom, Megan, my loving granddaughter.

Introduction

Giggles of Nature ...and Other Curious Wonders is a seamless sample of poetry in a most delicate presentation. This Christian author chooses some of her breeziest poems to entice the reader from the first page to the end of this pint-sized treasure. Her promise is sure to deliver a lilt to your step and a crisp sense of unrestrained pursuit of each page. For the reader who can receive only a morsel of verse at a time!

She may surprise you!

Table of Contents

SEASONS

THOUGHT-PROVOKING POESY

AUTUMN'S TANGO

Sundrenched autumn, strut your stuff.

Lift your leaves, flirtatious, bare-backed,

arched, victorious, to the tango wind.

Persimmon and strawberry-pink

inspire a melon-blush,

on a rust-spattered mountain-side canvas

and slip into sleep,

as dusk sweeps across a whisper.

In the hush of early morning,

the soft nudge of a wind-song summons:

"Yawn and stretch!" to waltz again at daybreak,

in the morning's crackling crisp.

GIGGLES OF NATURE

Gorgeous jade, appealing and luscious,

full and firm, poised for a photo!

I tip my hat and say,

"Much obliged."

Sassy sunflower, you!

Smiling coyly, stare toward

your worthy earth, then swift,

in step with the wind,

look to the sun; a lilt in your style

and a glimmer in your eye.

While walking on stones in my yard,

each dove wiggles his booty

-and chuckles as we pass.

Pudgy, fragile darlings!

LITTLE GIRL AT THE BEACH

"What do you see, Little Darlin'?"
Your tiny toes sinking into the ocean-wet earth.
As the sun's rays form diamonds on the sea,
the breeze hugs your tiny frame;
your mind swirls with wonder, under
your large brimmed hat.
What does the salty air taste like?
What dreams rush when grains of sand
fall between your little fingers?
All so new!
And oh, so grand!
As waves barely reach your ankles, you say,
"Mommy, a shell!
A penny! It's shiny!"
As waves play against the beach,
you pause…and say.
"Who's that face in the water, mommy?
Look -like you!? You?"
        "Julia, it's you, my Love."

THE POEM WRITER

The bard's voice surges

to sculpt a thought into wonder.

Words, wake up, from senses, misty with morning!

Rouse from sleep, or lazy minds

lose sight of happenings

that prod us to carve reflections on paper.

Words, dart forth with pen and ink!

And blaze!

QUIET MORNING

How still it is at first light,

    the birds whispering secrets.

The sound, sweet as honey, dripping.

    The breeze blends to offer background notes,

    soft and warm. God's melodic arrangement!

Here, in a sheltered setting, I inhale

    this exclusive recital.

SUMMER'S WIND SONG

Flowers dance at dawn.

The wind song,

far afield,

greets sunrise and foliage.

Small dewdrops part from wildflowers,

carefree, in pirouette and plié.

OCTOBER MORN

Drape your crimson-gold over my shoulders, your liquid emerald at my feet. Stay awhile and warm me with color before winter breaks the day with cold and ice.

October morn,

WAIT!

WAIT!!

WAIT!!

AUTUMN MERRIMENT

Fair Autumn, your majesty commands

first place among the seasons.

Speckled and spattered sun-gold

leaves drop recklessly,

showing off the dash of red

that highlights each fern as it falls.

They whirl like butterflies and flirt with wind gusts;

sway to the sky's refrain and whisk in the breeze.

They're playing, "Catch Me If You Can!"

A WOMAN'S JOY

It was winter, snowing, sun-shining and
morning, rising on a new life!

.

Thank you, for blessing me, dear Father,
on those two glorious mornings;

when the sun sparkled on the snow,
and I embraced the love of a child.

And I loved the child with a Mother's love
and a Woman's joy!

COUNTRYSIDE MINUET

All nature reels to the wind's minuet,
when that high-stepping breeze slows
to an air-breath, balanced, sweet and
welcome.

The grass leans in rhythm.

The blooms sway in time,
flaunting color and subtle balm.

Lizards dart to the next forage.

Fowls hide in nippy March.

But summer's song rouses robins to
trill sweet echoes in June -as flora and
fauna dance on.

PUZZLED

The wind whirls. Embraces me like a cloak!

I breathe the brisk of winter's cold.

Fingers numb, my eyes blink against the nip;
my tongue catches falling snowflakes.

With every step I hear the sound of ice,
crackling, echoing, then resting on footprints.
I walk a little further…

A breeze runs up my sleeve, chilling me,
and I feel, oh, so pleasurably ice-cold!!   Brrrrrrr!!

ANNIVERSARY – ROSE AND GEORGE

"Can this really be, George?
Does it seem like yesterday,
that we first smiled at love,
began our journey on life's way?
When hand in hand we strolled
down Lover's Lane, just you and I,
and vowed that through the years
our love, so true, would never die?"

"Well, Rosie, Doll, I think you're right,
no time it seems has passed.
We've toiled and loved
and dreamed and schemed,
so fervent at our task -
that suddenly we find
that fifty years have rolled on by.
Together we have known
a love that nothing could defy.
We've shared the sunshine and the rain
that life oft' brings to all.

I've concluded firmly,
"Only sunshine I recall."
The sunshine of the rainbow-colored
ribbons of our years
embroidered joys so radiant,
I can't recall the tears.

"I love you more today, my Rose
than words can 'ere bestow,
because the love light in your eyes
belongs to me alone."
"I love you more today,
dear George, than yesterday, it's true.
A friend, so kind and warm,
to walk life's path I've found in you.

Now, life has sprinkled memories
of our years together, dear;
with hopes of bright tomorrows,
with your love, ever near…"

MORNING SONG PRAISE

Lush leaves sweep the skies,
lifting my praises to God:
Thank You for morning!

In wind or stillness,
oaks lift their branches skyward!
Looks like praise to me!

SUNDAY AFTERNOON

The hastening prance of the
dancing wind is rich and full and free;
the presence of God is round about,
encircling, embracing me.
My baby's hand, so heather-new,
outstretched to reach my face.
With laughing eyes, my new-born child
is centered in God's embrace.
And the morn, on the breeze of a golden day,
yields a luster beyond compare;
and I'm hugged by my Lord
through the sights and the sounds
and the touch of the earth so fair.
By the giggles and starry-eyed wiles of kids and
by warmth and esteem of my friends;
for my life is held firm,
wrapped in God's warm embrace.
There I'll stay, resting safe in His love;
ever close,
resting warm in His love.

NIGHT IN SPRING

I'm here with you, Lord,

on this starry night,

listening to the ocean roar,

savoring salty air.

Mammoth waves emerge,

then quiet, flowing,

toward the sand to sleep.

Surrounded by your greatness, Lord,

this vast sea before me.

Your moon wants only to remain in this

moment and feel the wind's caress.

In awe, I stand before you, Lord.

Heaven and earth, displayed!

You are here, Lord,

   and I am filled

      with the wonder of Creation.

BREAK OF DAY

Silken rainbows ribbon across a
cerulean-blue heaven,
as lavish clouds break pink above
to celebrate homecoming.

She fills the house with dance
and sparkles glitter where she steps.
Waiting rooms breathe in fragrance.
Broken hearts are healed
and daybreak showers down a choir, singing.
Each room stands to applaud.

God's sky is mauve; the child is home,
and hugs are free.
And night is day.
And day breaks bright;
and sparkle shines in distant skies,
as purple plays on cotton candy clouds.

17

SWEET MOMENT IN TIME

Listen to the quiet.

This moment of solitude, unbroken,

with weeping willows swaying in sweet abandon

against an azure sky.

A cardinal struts nearby,

chirps a song written for me.

Rain droplets trickle down my cheeks.

The lazy morning sun enfolds me.

       Tomorrow will wait.

PRAYER AT DAYBREAK

Thank you for sunrise refrains
from birds who carol in the air.

The sky before morning stares down;
    sees my cactus bloom in December's frost
       -and ponders.

"How does it know, Lord?

Except, you speak?"

AT LAST, MY LOVE

When dawn boasts a plump, orange sun, I think of you.

When rains cascade at dusk or snowflakes sprinkle at morn and twilight flaunts the quarter moon, slender;

as music fills my room with the quiet essence of you, you fill my mind with playful shades of merry.

The musings of a million Eons unveil in these precise moments…

because your kiss was my awakening,

and I stirred, sublime, in your arms.

LOVE SONG

Two happy little kites, soaring,
dancing, entwined then, free-falling,
dancing earthward
-only to reach again, lazily toward the heavens,
like you and me in sheer abandon,
entwined, untwined, entwined again and again-
loving you, loving me.
At night in your arms,
you squeeze me as though it's the first time.

And the music plays on and on
into the autumn and winter of our years, together.

And we're dancing, free-falling,
then star-gazing,
reaching and soaring
toward heaven.

YESTERDAY, ACROSS A TABLE

Engaged in flatteries and flirtations,

a man and woman,

enamored with each other,

sit together at Gordon-Conwell

during a poetry workshop.

They are in their early sixties,

replaying my image of

my Love and me

in the autumn of our years.

I share the table with them and notice that

the woman wears my contentment in her eyes,

my joy in her smile.

She is his love-gift

and he is hers.

Pirouette and plie, like figurines

atop a jeweled music box, life is fragile.

The autumn years come swiftly.

Her husband caresses her

as though she were a porcelain doll.

Their eyes meet; their smiles greet.

This is first-love in autumn-time finery.

Now, I know: the tenderness I see in them

is the portrait others see in my Love and me.

Our eloquent look of love's exquisite love

 in autumn grandeur.

THE DANCE AND THE SMILE

I never bargained for Old Age.

Wrinkles - droopy jowls.

Blurred vision and the like.

But here it is,

falling boldly upon my face;

stamping its name, coldly – then

smirking – laughing.

Crotchety? Forgetful? Can't hear?

"Eh! What did you say, Sonny?"

I never bargained for Old Age,

slipping in insidiously.

I never said O.K. to this deal.

We never shook hands over it and agreed.

No. It just stomped in boldly;

took hold and-wiped out the young days!

As though it had the right.

I never said it did, but here it is.

And now? Cope with this?!

As though life's struggle were not enough

to mold and to refine! I find this Unwelcomed Guest racing around my bend.

There, at the door of my days; greeting me with its own inimitable stance.

Just there…Dare I embrace this unfamiliar cloak of time?

Dare I not?

I'll dance old age a waltz.

And smile old age a lullaby.

A CURIOUS STATE OF GRACE

Never thought about it much till now, you know…this -timeline. Ah, splendid youth and fluid movement, quick and sure, without pause. Hour-glass figure, skin, taut; stance, confident… catapulting into a curious state of grace.

Almond-shaped, brown eyes, beautiful and bright, grow tired; eyesight dims, hearing halves, stature shrinks; yet a state of grace, nonetheless, curious as it may be, where steps are slow, labored, deliberate.

Even though others welcome my wisdom, I never thought about change much, till now…the way change occurs, ever so slowly, every day, bit by bit, diminishing me a tad –depleting me.
This body of mine wears itself out!! And one day will wither and die, yes. True.

Today, though, before that day comes:
my laughter is welcomed in rooms where I enter,
and my warmth received by those who gather at
my table or in my yard...
I am at peace with who I am, and Whose I am;
where I've been -and where I'm going.

I am content to look toward heaven and
remember His promise. He remains my Portion,
who breathes life into each new day. And softly, I
say, "Stay with me, Lord, as I grow older, and with
joy, await your return."

WONDER OF WONDERS

What compares with the course of human Birth?

Feeling your baby stretching, turning, punching, kicking inside of you! How can this be!?

The splendor of life inside the womb before life takes its place after birth!

Then, at last, beholding the child in your arms!

Little pitter-patter package wrapped in blankets, warm…

And wonder of wonders, as years go by, you picture your child's face in his child's smile.

ABOUT THE AUTHOR

Carol Ann Castagna is a Christian poetess, composer and lyricist, published author, pianist and retired psychiatric R.N. Clinician. She graduated Bridgeport Hospital School of Nursing, then earned her Bachelor of Science Degree in Social Services from the University of Bridgeport and pursued graduate studies in Art Therapy at Albertus Magnus College. She has held positions from Staff Nurse to Director of Nursing Services in her chosen field over the course of 25 years. She was especially fond of working in the community and in the E.R. where she evaluated patients diagnostically and recommended levels of care and treatment follow-up. She loved as well, her years as Head Nurse in the Adolescent Psychiatric Hospital in Newtown, CT.

Carol's writings have been published in several publications including the book, *Penned from the Heart,* Nursing Spectrum, Connecticut Nursing News, and "Poetry Pacific," an e-zine, as well as several anthologies. Many of her poems were entered in contests and received Honorable Mention by her peers, including the Senior Poet Laureate and the Editors and Writers Network. Almost a dozen poems were displayed for two consecutive years, 1999 and 2000 by the Komen Ct Art for the Cure at the New Britain Museum of American Art. The Author is a member of Word Weavers, International, The North Port Art Center, The North Port Writers Workshop and The Allamanda Garden Club, where she has read her poems to the audiences. She is the author of her first book, *A Gentle Kiss from God: A Devotional in Free Verse,* an illustrated book of prayer, praise, poetry and music that alludes to her own life's story.

An accomplished pianist, Carol has used her talents to delight and uplift patients at hospitals, assisted living lodgings and hospices. She has served as church pianist most of her life and has also taught piano. The music of her original compositions can be accessed on her website http:// www.joypsalms.com: her lyrics can be found under the Poetry tab of same.

Carol's inspirational Christian blog includes Scripture, original writings and piano music. All of this, a testament to her love for her Savior, Jesus Christ. Carol considers the Lord's gifts an enormous blessing—and desires to share them with you. She humbly presents her e-book and printed version of poetry, *Giggles of Nature …and Other Curious Wonders* to you. She is married to the Rev. Vincent Castagna. Their blended family consists of four children, eight grandchildren, three greatgrandchildren, and one on the way! They make their home near the Gulf Coast of Florida.

.

Find it on Amazon and other book sites: *Giggles of Nature ...and Other Curious Wonders*

https://www.facebook.com/Mrs.Rev.VC/

Author's website: www.joypsalms.com

ACKNOWLEDGMENTS

Thank you, Megan, for your lovely artwork that graces the cover of *Giggles of Nature…and Other Curious Wonders.* To Vincent, my dear husband, for seeing me through the arduous task of crafting a book and for effecting the technological aspects of the project.

Many *thanks* to Lisa Ashley, for formatting *Giggles of Nature…and Other Curious Wonders* for KDP and paperback.